9ONLINE

BUSINESS IDEAS

THAT WILL *STILL BE HUGE*

IN 2016

FROM A SIX FIGURE
INTERNET ENTREPRENEUR

Bonus! - As a way of saying thanks, here's a short book that is guaranteed to excel your business career. It helped me greatly and will do the same for you if you can internalise the concepts.

Download Here → *http://goo.gl/iYx5aC*

9 ONLINE BUSINESS IDEAS THAT WILL STILL BE HUGE IN 2016

From a SIX Figure Internet Entrepreneur

Written By:

Mateen S

Brought to you by AffEngineer.com

www.AffEngineer.com Copyright © 2015 by AffEngineer Publishing

Disclaimer

9 Online Business ideas that will still be huge in 2016

Making money on the internet has been around for a long time. The problem is, quality information gets lost amongst an ocean of ebooks and courses that make huge promises but teach you very little. It took me a long time to filter out the bad and find the good. Many times I had to just grind it out and find out for myself whether or not a method works.

I've been in the scene full-time for almost 3 years now and have made money via a variety of different ways. From blogging to affiliate marketing to FaceBook Pages, I've had the chance to try and compare many money making endeavours online.

Some have failed, some have bought in a couple hundred, some have gone on to make me six figures within a year. The potential to make money on the internet is massive. This holds true now more than ever as profitable businesses are turning towards a more web and tech based approach.

In this book, I'll go through 9 of them. I know they work because either I've tried them myself or I know someone who has. Either way, there is someone out there making a living doing it.

Contrary to popular ebooks that post pictures of people on the beaches of the Bahamas sipping out of a freshly cut coconut, I'm going to tell you that online business is hard. It's very possible but takes more determination and persistence than just a few weekends. If you're willing to give it 3-6 months of consistent work and a healthy experimental budget, then the online world is your oyster [and through trial and error you'll most definitely find something that works for you.

I can write 10,000 Words on each one of

the below techniques but for the sake of keeping this book short and simple to follow, I'm going to touch upon each one briefly. Take them as a starting point as to the possibilities and potential of the tech world.I consistently experiment with different techniques and share case studies, tips and financial data with my Insider list. Join Here → http://goo.gl/jQn9ou

Table of Contents

1. Blogging

Blogging is the first idea that comes to mind. It's not new and has been around for over a decade. Blogging is the simple process of creating a website about a particular topic and publishing a piece of writing on the blog ever so often.

AffEngineer.com is my blog. I started it about 2 years ago with the intent to mind dump thoughts and strategies I would come across in my day-to-day business activities. I never intended to make money from it. Two years later and it's earned me over 50k and continues to bring me a healthy monthly salary.

Over time people started to find my website, ask questions, request for ebooks and more information. I directed them to resources that had helped me and so I knew they would help them. It was all a natural 'non-salesy' process that happened without pushing for it.

It's also the most maintenance free part of my overall business. I'll work a couple of hours a week tops to maintain a good monthly income. Yes, I'll do the occasional 1 week straight sprints, making an ebook or a set of YouTube tutorial videos but for the most part, it's a stress free, cost effective method to make money online.

Some notable blogs you can go through are,

SmartPassiveIncome
Digital Photography School
AffEngineer
PsyBlog

Over time people who manage these blogs gain a following and as they write more and market themselves, this following continues to grow. They'll monetise their blogs by selling ad space, selling products through recommendations, selling ebooks, etc.

I'm sure you come across interesting articles on blogs at least a few times a week. Next time you're on one, look around and try spot different types of marketing techniques. From immediate opt-in pop ups to small ads in the corner, each blog or websites has different ways of making money.

A blog isn't that difficult to start and I started mine with 0 knowledge of coding or website creation. Everything you need to know to get started is on YouTube somewhere and can be learned over a few weekends. People have made YouTube tutorials about absolutely everything and there definitely is no shortage of blogger tutorials.

The process of making money through blogging is a different story. It involves implementing marketing techniques that bring you quality web traffic who are willing to spend money if you can prove to them your product has value. Your product can be something physical or something digital like an ebook. Selling will come natural if you're honest and provide value to the people that read it. If you really have quality information to share, people can sense it.

The costs involved with blogging compared to the income potential of it is great. It's one of the best in the online industry. I spend a couple hundred dollars a month to maintain my blog and it brings me a healthy 3-4k, sometimes even more. For many others, their ROI is much bigger!

The costs involved are,

Domain Name: This is the usability rights of the name you choose to call your website. Eg, www.Jennystips.com or www.bloghelper.com. You can call it anything you want as long as the name itself is not taken. This costs around $10 - $20/year.

Host: A Host is basically an online hard-drive where the data from your website is stored. Things like pictures, text, videos, scripts and other data that a website requires is stored on a server or host. Hosting accounts can cost $5/month to $1000s/month. At the beginning, a simple hosting account at around $5 a month is fine. Bluehost can provide this and they also give you one free domain name of your choice!

That's basically it! Everything else is optional. Sometimes I pay for advertising spots and blog post trades. There are plenty of ways to go around marketing your blog but for now the best thing to do is make one and get the hang of updating it. Again, it's a lot easier than most people think! Think of it like learning how to use Microsoft PowerPoint or Microsoft Word.

The simplest way to get started with this is to use a software called 'Wordpress'.

Wordpress makes it very easy for simple people with 0 coding experience to create beautiful blogs. It's used by almost every blogger. When you register with Bluehost and have your domain name ready you can install wordpress on your account. It's all on YouTube for anyone that doesn't know how to do this or you can get Bluehost support to help you out for free.

I've written a slightly more in-depth article about starting a blog here. Check it out if you're interested in this idea. Matthew Woodward does a great job of monetising his blog. He also posts monthly income reports on exactly how he goes about doing it. Read up on his blog if you want to see blogging in action and want further information as to how this model works.

2. Instagram

Instagram has become one of the most popular social media sites in the world. With it's simplicity and ease of use, no wonder many people use it but how can this platform make us money?

Any website that brings a lot of traffic will eventually become a platform where money can be earned. Remember this as a general rule. The reason why websites like FaceBook, Instagram and Whatsapp are worth so much is because of their _user base._ A small announcement on FaceBook and most of the western world will know about it. Can you imagine how important and valuable this can be for marketing companies who's goal is to reach as many people as they can?

With Instagram you can start accounts about a particular topic, let's say 'Mens

Fashion'.

You can post pictures of fashionable items every day and grow your Instagram following to something considerable, usually above 50k. After you reach a size that has a decent out reach people will start approaching you to advertise their brands and products through your account.
The same way social celebrities often get approached to wear clothes on behalf of brands that want to market themselves, you can post images that are beneficial to companies for a small fee.

I've spent $20 for someone to post out something for me before and it's worked well. I know accounts that make their yearly salary this way. People spend $1000's on just one post from a popular Instagram account. It's reported that Kim Kardashian makes $10k per tweet! You can imagine how much she'd make per Instagram post! It's not a new concept and has been around for a while. You can do the same thing with FaceBook Pages, Pinterest boards and twitter.

Before you embark on your social media empire, just know that you need to be patient and consistent with the initial posting and growing of your account. It takes time to build something valuable enough to be used by others. If you're willing to give it 6 months to a year then go for it. It will only get easier in time and you can start using your large accounts to jump start your newer accounts.

Here is a great thread on WarriorForum where someone has explained how they make 2-$300 a day on Instagram.

3. Kindle Publishing

Kindle is Amazons eBook selling platform. Amazon is an absolute giant in terms of online selling and sells pretty much everything you can think of. From toys to swimming pools to furniture, there's hardly anything that Amazon does not sell.

Something you may not know about Amazon is that most of their products come from other companies and small home business owners who use Amazon to sell their products.

For example if I had a small pet shop. I can list my products on Amazon and once they make sales, simply send it to whomever made the purchase. Amazon will take a cut and you'll make your profit.

Their kindle space does the same thing. People like me and you can 'publish' books on any topic and Amazon will use it's power to market your books if it's doing better than others and you'll makes sales from it. There are some popular bloggers who have made 5 figures a month doing this.

Steve Scott is one of them.

Kindle publishing is a great way to make money as long as you are consistent and informative with your kindle books.

Remember, it's not as easy as just publishing your book on Kindle. That's just the first step. You need to use some marketing techniques to push sales so that Amazon will identify it as something 'hot', and will begin to bundle market it with other Amazon products.

If you like writing and have a wealth of knowledge on a certain topic to share, this one may be for you. Mind you, you have to be comfortable with writing 5-20k words per book or in the case of fiction writing even more!

I hated writing. English was my worst subject at school but when I started to write about what I liked and enjoyed, it became much easier. At school we're forced to write about topics we don't really care about which is the reason it's hard to hit essay word counts. I write 2-4,000 words a day for my kindle books and much of it just flows out from my fingers with ease as it's something I've dedicated my whole career to.

Steve Scott goes through how he makes money on Kindle. He has loads of tips and tricks for anyone that wants to get started in this business.

4. Phone Applications

Phone applications will always be around.
Since the first iPhone has hit the market,
the Phone application space has become a
gold mine for savvy entrepreneurs. From
developers to designers to people who
know nothing about the above, phone apps
have made a lot of people a lot of money.

It's never too late to jump in and get a piece
of the pie. Where there's thriving
competition, there's plenty of people to
serve so don't be intimidated by the fact
that others have a bigger head start to you.
Believe in yourself, it will take you far.

I've made a couple of phone apps before.
I've made hundreds of dollars on my first
app and I'm sure if I had continued with my
phone app journey, I would have made
plenty more money.

I knew nothing about coding and nothing

about design. In fact, I learned the basics of photoshop in 2 weekends watching YouTube videos just so I could make mock up designs of how I wanted my phone app to look.

Again, almost everything can be learned from YouTube so don't worry if you don't know something.

I used elance.com to find a developer over seas that was willing to make my app for $200. As my first app, I didn't want to spend too much money. This turned out to be a great decision as it was perfect to test the waters and I soon realised I had a LOT to learn.

Too many people spend more than they can afford to lose with their business ventures which is why, in most cases, they give up. Business is difficult at the start and it takes a bunch of failures for your mind to start adjusting to what works and what doesn't. Don't spend so much that it's hard to recover from your failures. The quicker you make your mistakes, the quicker you'll learn. Just make sure you can recover from them.

Give yourself that time and space to learn from your mistakes.

Phone apps are great and exciting and I recommend anyone to give it a go. You don't have to be the next Instagram or Pinterest, even a small to medium sized app can make you a healthy yearly income.

I recommend Chad Muretas Appreneur book if your interested. It gave me a lot of insight into the app world and what I'd need to do to get into it.

Phone apps make money a variety of different ways. From selling ad space which is simply embedding pieces of coding within the app pages so that Google or another company can display ads.

You can sell a paid version of the app, you can sell in app purchases, (which work great!). There are plenty of ways to go about this.

The app space is very much like the kindle space. You'll have to give it that initial boost of marketing but once that's done, the app store or play store will do it's job of marketing you within their top rankings, increasing your visibility to potential customers. It may take you a few apps to learn the dynamics of all this but I assure you, you'll get there as long as you continue with it.

5. Fiverr

Fiverr is an interesting income idea.

Although I use it mainly to get small tasks done, many people make a decent part time income from Fiverr.

Fiverr.com is a website that allows you to post a job or 'gig' about any topic. Some example gigs are,

- Hold up a sign with words of your choice
- Sing a birthday song with the name of your choice
- Draw a cartoon picture of your photo
- etc

There are 3 million different gigs as mentioned on wikipedia, as of this moment, with people ready to do all kinds of small tasks for $5. It's a great website to use if you're building your own website and require small tasks to be done.

A couple of ways to make money through Fiverr is to become a freelancer yourself and list your own gig. Yes, there is quite a lot of competition that's why you need to be able to provide something with your own twist. Don't just do the same thing everyone else is doing, I can't see you getting many orders with 100's of others providing the exact same thing.

Another way is to find work on elance or odesk. These are freelancing websites that works similar to Fiverr except it's not limited to just $5. People post their online project requirements which later receive bids or proposals from contractors who are ready to do this sort of work.

You can find some Fiverr gigs that are able to do the same tasks on the above two websites for $5. Some tasks can be logo design, small SEO services, small development jobs, etc. There are 100s of available tasks that can be done.

You can become the intermediary consultant who gets work from elance and finds Fiverr gigs to fulfil these orders and take a cut in between as your profit margin. It's referred to as arbitrage in the financial world and many companies employ this tactic. Buy from a cheaper market and sell to a more expensive one.

If you feel like there are a lot of great small services you may be able to offer people on the internet, try Fiverr.

6. eBay

eBay is another giant that has been around for a long time. I remember being in school and people would tell me they got their gameboy off eBay and I'd be astonished at how cheap they were able to buy things for.

I used eBay all through my school and university years to buy and sell things for profit. I'd buy from eBay and sell on eBay. Simple things like just changing the item from international to local can allow you to sell it for 3 times more!

I was buying digital watches for $4 from eBay international and selling them on eBay Australia for $15. Making a healthy $5-$10 profit on each one. It's astonishing how many things you can buy and sell.

As you keep trying, you keep learning and little tips and tricks like these, that no one really knows about, can make you a lot of cash.

I would recommend eBay for people that enjoy the thrill of buying and selling. I've been addicted to buying and selling for a long time and the idea of creating wealth from pretty much nothing challenges me.

You can even buy from eBay and sell from Gumtree or Craigslist. Or vice versa. All you're trying to do here is find people who are selling it for less and people who are willing to buy it for more.

There is plenty of money to be made so jump in and start trading! It definitely takes some time to start learning what works well. You won't get it right straight off the bat. Try look for other markets where you can buy items. Alibaba is a good one although with its growing popularity things aren't as cheap as they used to be.

Make a spreadsheet of everything you've bought and sold. Make sure you account for all costs involved so you know exactly what your profit margins are. From petrol to drive to the post office to small post office items, account for everything! You don't want to be deluded with how much money you seem to be making.

7. Affiliate Marketing

Affiliate Marketing has been my bread and butter for a long time. It's the process of selling products on behalf of another company and obtaining a commission for your efforts. It's basically a commission based marketer but in the online world.

Most likely you would have bought something from an Affiliate Marketer and wouldn't have even realised.

All of 2014 I sold Custom Apparel on behalf of Teespring, a major apparel manufacturer. I sold over half a million dollars worth of Apparel and pocketed a healthy 6 figures in profit.

My activities included designing the prints and using FaceBook marketing to drive interested traffic who followed through to purchase the product I was advertising.

I'd spend $30 for 100 people to visit the merchant store for each item out of which around 4-5% would follow through with a purchase making me a healthy profit. This didn't happen for every design. Often, 1 out of 20 would bring me a profit, the rest would be fails.

This is the reality of the online business world. It's all a numbers game. Don't just try 1 or 2 times at something. Try it 50 times. Literally. It took me 50 designs to find one that sold when I first started with Teespring. I could have quit after 5 but I didn't. I kept moving forward knowing that this is what I needed to do to figure it all out.

Affiliate marketing is mostly about managing your costs with your revenue and ensuring you're making a profit. You have to spend a lot of money so it's definitely not for the faint hearted and risk averse.

It's a great skill to learn though. How and

where to spend money on online marketing methods that can boost sales towards your business. You become extremely valuable to businesses and they can treat you to gifts and increase your payouts.

You will have a much better fighting chance if you ever decide to start your own business some day. Most people just start a business and have no idea on how to market it. They don't know where to spend their money or efforts and are too immersed in just making everything look pretty to focus on the main task at hand. The task of making money.

There are plenty of affiliate marketing blogs out there that share the exact way they make money. Popular ones I know of include,

Charlesngo.con
AffEngineer.com (Mine)
Tylercruz.com (Read some of his older posts)

NickyCakes.com

If you're really serious, I'd recommend joining a paid marketing forum like <u>Aff Playbook</u>. It's filled with affiliate marketers who share their experiences and help each other get to the point they want to be. I started there when I was a total newbie and had my first $200+ profit product a few months later.

8. Email Marketing

Email marketing is the process of gathering peoples emails to provide them with value and to sell them the occasional product or service. There are people making a LOT of money email marketing to people.

It's been around for decades and many people have found themselves on the list of an email marketer.

There are too many people doing this wrong. In a way that provides little to no value and comes off as spammy. I don't recommend this method. In fact if you're going to do that, I'd prefer you skip this one.

You want to provide your email list with value. They've opted in and trusted you with their email. The last thing you should do is spam them with links to random things. Send them helpful articles, things you've found that they can relate to. Information that you would personally spend time reading. Pretend your mother or father or close relative is on that list. What would you send them? And more importantly <u>what wouldn't</u> you send them?

Every now and then mention a product that you would actually buy yourself. Make a recommendation and link to the product with your affiliate link.

Again, I know people making quite a lot of people with this and it definitely works.

The hard part is to generate the list. There are many ways to do this and I've been able to generate a list in the 10s of thousands by using FaceBook marketing.

Other ways are to have a website, bait people with an ebook and get them to opt-in to receive it. This is the most common, but may take a while as you're waiting for traffic to come through.

Services like Aweber and Mailchimp allow you to manage your email lists. They provide analytical data on how your lists are responding to mail outs such as how many are clicking on links, your open rates, complaint rates etc.

It's best to know how to build simple Wordpress websites too so you can direct people to your online stores or blogs, further increasing your traffic and interaction.

9. Adsense

Adsense is a popular form of internet monetisation that most website owners use to make money form their websites.

It's probably the easiest way to make money but it's very difficult to make anything decent unless you have a high amount of quality traffic coming in.

Adsense is basically Googles way of advertising on your website. You would have seen plenty of Adsense ads in your life time.

Bloggers and other website owners place a code on their website which allows Google to generate visual ads like the above. These ads are made by companies who use Google as an advertising platform. Google selects sites on their behalf that are related to the interests of these companies and will generate the ad on your site.

As people click on these ads, Google charges these companies and you get a small cut out of what Google makes in profit.

For example, if I wanted to promote a shirt that I made geared at dog lovers. I'll select dog lovers as the interest group and Google will find me dog lover websites that have Adsense installed in them. Every person that sees this ad and clicks on it will be directed to my website and the website owner who displayed my ad on behalf of Google will be paid by Google for getting someone to click my ad.

The same thing applies with YouTube. Companies pay YouTube a fee for every click YouTube generates them on their website.

You can make money this way by making a website with a lot of traffic and installing

Adsense. Adsense should't really be used as the only monetisation strategy which in most case will limit the amount of money you make. Most people use Adsense in conjunction with selling ebooks and other things.

Many Popular FaceBook pages will try get you to click on links that take you to their website. They'll hope for people to click on ads around their site so they can generate money. Pages that have millions of fans can generate quite a lot of money on their Websites.

The idea is to make a website that shares information on a niche that people like. It can be a blog, a forum, a simple game site, something that generates a high quantity of web traffic. Once you place Adsense ads strategically around your website, people will start clicking on these ads which will generate you revenue.

Adsense is one of the most common ways

of making money on the internet and if you were to do a simple search on making money with Adsense, you'll find tonnes of case studies and information.

Conclusion

The above methods have been found out by observing small things I've come across every now and then and putting ideas into practice. Every time you are marketed to online, try and find out why or how that person is making money. There might be opportunity for you to jump in and make money yourself.

All of these ideas can make you money so just pick one and stick to it. It's not easy and will take a lot of work and persistence but as long as you stick with it you'll see results.

These ideas are proven to work. They're not just ideas but are actual money making models that someone else around the world is using to make their income.

These people are no different to you,

they've just been in the game longer. The quicker you get started, the quicker you'll get there so pick something and go for it.

Lastly, don't forget to get onto our Insider List! I share case studies of the above ideas and tips on entrepreneurship that have made me money.

Join Here → http://goo.gl/wcNCvW

Good luck!

Mateen S

Join Over 1,000 People in our Insider List

Insiders get Business Case Studies, Income Reports, the below upcoming Book Titles for free upon launch and much much more!

Join Here → *http://goo.gl/jQn9ou*

<u>COMING SOON</u>

Author Bio

Mateen has loved entrepreneurship since school. Buying and selling USB's, phones and game consoles on eBay and Gumtree, he learned the art of the hustle young.

Two years into his engineering career he quit to dedicate himself to entrepreneurship and take it to the next level.

Three years since the day he's quit from work life, he's made six figures from a variety of different entrepreneurship avenues. From selling merchandise on the famous Teespring platform to blogging. He's blog, affengineer.com, has been featured on prominent websites and is known to be the best for Teespring information.

He dedicates himself to finding ways to make money and sharing it with his insider list to create a community comfortable with sharing information and helping each other get to the financial place they desire.

If you would like to be part of the insider list, join below.

http://goo.gl/jQn9ou

www.ingramcontent.com/pod-product-compliance
Lightning Source LLC
Chambersburg PA
CBHW051224170526
45166CB00005B/2036